INTO BATTLE!

Written by Adam Bray

Penguin
Random
House

Editors Emma Grange, Gaurav Joshi
Art Editors Karan Chaudhary, Pallavi Kapur
DTP Designers Umesh Singh Rawat, Rajdeep Singh
Pre-Production Producer Siu Yin Chan
Pre-Production Manager Sunil Sharma
Producer Louise Daly
Managing Editors Simon Hugo, Chitra Subramanyam
Managing Art Editors Neha Ahuja, Guy Harvey
Art Director Lisa Lanzarini
Publisher Julie Ferris
Publishing Director Simon Beecroft

Reading Consultant Linda B. Gambrell, Ph.D

Dorling Kindersley would like to thank Randi Sørensen, Paul Hansford,
and Robert Stefan Ekblom at the LEGO Group.

For Lucasfilm
Executive Editor Jonathan W. Rinzler
Art Director Troy Alders
Story Group Rayne Roberts, Pablo Hidalgo, Leland Chee

First American Edition, 2015
Published in the United States by DK Publishing
345 Hudson Street, New York, New York 10014

Page design copyright © 2015 Dorling Kindersley Limited
A Penguin Random House Company
15 16 17 18 19 10 9 8 7 6 5 4 3 2 1
001–279488–July/2015

A catalog record for this book is available from the Library of Congress.
ISBN: 978-1-4654-3621-4 (Hardback)
ISBN: 978-1-4654-3534-7 (Paperback)

DK books are available at special discounts when purchased in bulk for
sales promotions, premiums, fund-raising, or educational use.
For details, contact: DK Publishing Special Markets,
345 Hudson Street, New York, New York 10014
SpecialSales@dk.com

Printed and bound in China

www.LEGO.com
www.starwars.com
www.dk.com

A WORLD OF IDEAS:
SEE ALL THERE IS TO KNOW

Contents

Galaxy in Conflict

The galaxy is a big and dangerous place, full of powerful forces and individuals. Many people live in peace, but sometimes that peace must be won in battle. Others want to create wars, and do all they can to make trouble.

The most powerful people in the galaxy draw their strength from an energy called the Force. The light side of the Force is a power

for good, and is used by wise peacekeepers called the Jedi. They believe in learning and reason, wear simple robes, and defend their way of life with weapons called lightsabers.

But the Force also has a dark side, which is used by evildoers called the Sith. They are hungry for power at any cost and use lies as well as weapons in their attempts to control the galaxy. The Sith hate the Jedi and use lightsabers of their own to fight them!

The Jedi have many friends to help
them fight evil. In the days of the Galactic
Republic, there were many Jedi, including
Obi-Wan Kenobi and Qui-Gon Jinn. When
the Sith threatened this peaceful Republic,
brave individuals such as Senator Padmé
Amidala and General Jar Jar Binks stood
alongside the Jedi in battle.

Later, when the Sith ruled the galaxy as
an Empire, only a handful of Jedi remained,
like Kanan Jarrus on the planet Lothal and

Luke Skywalker on Tatooine. But they could count on the help of the Rebel Alliance— a band of daring freedom-fighters including Han Solo, Chewbacca, and Princess Leia.

The Sith do not have any friends, but trick others into doing their dirty work. They can command vast armies of droids, or conquer a planet with their wits alone.

As rebels stand with Jedi and battle droids line up with Sith Lords, the stage is set to go into battle!

KNOW YOUR WARRIORS
JEDI

The Force is strong in the Jedi, but unlike the Sith they use it to protect the galaxy and its people. Their weapon of choice is the glowing lightsaber.

MASTER
YODA

PHYSICAL ANALYSIS

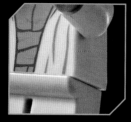

STRONG SENSES

Jedi ears are sensitive to the faintest of noises.

ROBES

Loose robes help them in meditating and for Force jumps in battle!

"DO. OR DO NOT. THERE IS NO TRY."
Yoda

WEAPON OF CHOICE

Jedi often carry green or blue lightsabers. They are experts in combat skills. A true Jedi will wield his lightsaber only to defend, not to destroy.

90%
BATTLE SKILLS

KNOWN FOR Selfless service

ALLEGIANCE Light side of the Force

PERSONALITY Even-tempered

ENEMIES The Sith

STRENGTH Wisdom, the Force

WEAKNESS Overconfidence

WATCH OUT FOR Jedi mind tricks!

• BATTLE STORY •

Jedi don't equate size with power and strength. Grand Master Yoda is known for his whirlwind fighting style. Once, Yoda was attacked by strong, experienced clone troopers on Kashyyyk. He destroyed them quickly with his lightsaber.

Ground Battles

In the struggle for control of the galaxy, what happens on the ground can be just as important as what happens in space. Armies march over long distances to fight on many different terrains: from open fields on the planet Naboo, to Endor's dense forests, sandy deserts on Tatooine, and Hoth's snowy wastelands.

In his quest to gain absolute power, the evil Sith Lord Darth Sidious starts huge ground battles on many planets. Win or lose, he always finds a way to profit!

When war comes to a planet, the people who live there must choose whether to fight or flee. If they fight, they must pick a side! Heroes such as hairy Wookiee Chewbacca and clumsy Gungan Jar Jar Binks fight against the forces of Darth Sidious. Villains like Nute Gunray and Poggle the Lesser side with the powerful Sith.

It is on the Great Grass Plains of the planet Naboo that Darth Sidious first orders a ground invasion. Sidious was born on Naboo, where he went by the name of Palpatine and pretended to be a kind politician. He forces the greedy Trade Federation to invade his own planet with battle droids as part of his plan to gain more power for himself!

Yet Naboo is also home to the proud Gungans, including the clumsy but kind-hearted Jar Jar Binks. Armed with blue booma bombs, they fight bravely against the droid army, even though they are badly outnumbered. Luckily, the battle droids have one major weakness: They are all controlled from one spaceship. When that ship is blown up by young hero Anakin Skywalker, all the droids stop in their tracks. In fact, they stop doing anything at all! The Gungans have won and Naboo is peaceful again.

FACE-OFF
Gungan Warrior vs. War Machine

It's time for Jar Jar Binks to face his fear and defend Naboo. Will the nasty battle droids beat him?

"Wesa got a grand army!"

Jar Jar Binks, Gungan Warrior

- **Strength** Loyal to his tribe
- **Weakness** Easily scared
- **Weapons** Booma, assault cannons

Battle Droid, War Machine

- **Strength** Feels no pain or fear
- **Weakness** Limited intelligence
- **Weapon** Blaster rifle

"Open fire!"

Ten years after the Battle of Naboo, young Anakin Skywalker is in trouble again! As part of his training to become a Jedi, he travels to the rocky, desert planet of Geonosis with Padmé Amidala to rescue his friend Obi-Wan Kenobi. There they are taken prisoner by the planet's ruler, Poggle the Lesser. Mean Poggle is working for an evil Sith Lord named Count Dooku and wants to feed Anakin, Obi-Wan, and Padmé to his fearsome arena beasts!

Fortunately, Poggle's plan is foiled when an army of 200 Jedi arrive, led by brave Jedi Master Mace Windu. But it's no easy win. An enormous battle begins when the Jedi come under attack from Super Battle Droids, which are bigger and scarier than the droids fought by the Gungans on Naboo! It looks as if the droids can't lose, but the Jedi have one more surprise for them: a vast army of clone troopers led by Jedi Master Yoda. The droids are defeated!

The Battle of Geonosis was the start of the Clone Wars—three years of fighting to decide whether light or darkness would control the galaxy. The Battle of Kashyyyk is one of the last battles in the Clone Wars. It doesn't go well for the Jedi!

When Master Yoda arrives on the planet Kashyyyk to help fight a droid invasion, the clone army he leads is fiercely loyal to him. They join forces with the tall, hairy Wookiee warriors that live there and together they fight the droids. Using three-legged AT-AP walkers, eight-wheeled turbo tanks, and flying ornithopters, they look set to beat the droids. But the Jedi are betrayed! Still pretending to be good, Sidious is now Supreme Chancellor of the Galactic Republic and can give orders to the clones, even though they are under Yoda's command. Sidious tells them to carry out Order 66—destroy all Jedi! The clones turn on the Jedi. Yoda is one of the few to escape. Now the dark side rules the galaxy.

  After the Battle of Kashyyyk, Darth
Sidious becomes the supreme ruler of the
galaxy. Calling himself Emperor, he controls
a huge army of stormtroopers and Imperial
weapons. He seems so powerful and
unstoppable that when a group of brave
rebels unites to fight him, they are hoping
only to dent his power, not defeat his empire
entirely. So when stormtroopers attack the
rebel base on the snowy world of Hoth, the
rebels are fighting to survive, not to win.

In order to cope with the cold of Hoth, the stormtroopers wear special snowtrooper armor and travel in AT-ATs: massive, four-legged walking weapons that can march across any terrain. But these legs are also a weakness. The AT-ATs can be tripped up! A group of rebels flies their snowspeeders around the AT-ATs, wrapping their legs in strong cables and making them fall over! This bravery gives their friends time to get away. But they will have to find a new base!

When the Empire destroyed the rebel base on Hoth, they won the battle, but the rebels lived to fight another day. The next big ground battle between them achieves what seemed impossible: the defeat of the Empire once and for all!

Above the forest moon of Endor, the Emperor rules the galaxy from a vast space station and weapon known as the Death Star. It is protected by an energy shield projected from the moon's surface.

On the forest moon, the rebel heroes team up with the small furry Ewoks who live there to attack the shield generator. It is heavily guarded by stormtroopers, but the Ewoks are not afraid. They use homemade spears and catapults to defeat their unwelcome visitors. Han Solo blows up the generator, meaning the Death Star can be destroyed by the rebel fleet in space. Then the Ewoks and rebels can celebrate together!

Let the WOOKiEE win! A guide to battle tactics by Chewbacca

Rule 1: ALWAYS WIN

As a Wookiee, it is very important always to be the winner in any conflict. If you aren't, growl until everyone agrees that you definitely are.

Rule 2: NEVER LOSE

Another very important habit of highly effective Wookiees is never to be the loser in any conflict. For more information, refer to rule 1.

Chief Tarfful says: "I learned everything I know about bashing droids from Chewbacca's great guide to battle tactics!"

Battles in Space

In the vast emptiness of
space, battles can be any size,
and danger can come from any
direction! Darth
Sidious feels right at
home in this cold and
dark setting, and space
battles are a big part of his
plans to control more and
more of the galaxy.

It's not just battles that can
be very big in space. Spaceships
can be enormous, and Sidious
and his dark side allies have
the biggest of them all. The
terrifying Super Star Destroyer
stretches several miles from one end to
the other, while the mighty Death Star
is the same size as a small planet!

The heroes that do battle with the dark
side cannot hope to fly such big ships,

so they rely on speed and skill. Working together, expert pilots like Wedge Antilles and Luke Skywalker, in one-person starfighters such as X-wings and Naboo's ships, can inflict a surprising amount of damage on even the biggest of the Empire's battleships—as we are about to find out!

Sometimes, a battle can be won by happy accident! Earlier we saw how the ground battle on the planet Naboo was won when young Anakin Skywalker blew up the spaceship controlling the army of droids below. But how exactly did he do it?

Anakin comes from the planet Tatooine, where he was famous for his skill as a pilot in a very scary sport called podracing. So when he finds himself on Naboo, hiding from

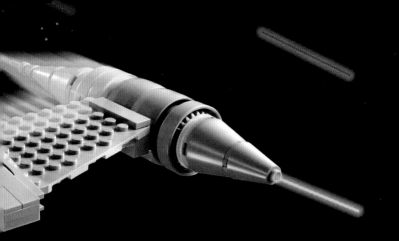

danger in the pilot's seat of a bright yellow
starfighter, it's no suprise that he feels right
at home! He launches the ship by mistake
and the autopilot flies him straight into the
heart of a space battle. Anakin's ship is soon
overwhelmed by swarming vulture droids,
and seeks refuge inside the very ship that is
controlling the droids down on Naboo.

As Anakin tries to get his ship up and
running again, he accidentally fires a shot
from its weapons system—destroying the
Droid Control Ship's power source! He is
able to fire up his engines just in time to
escape, not even knowing that he has ended
a battle! The Force works in marvelous ways.

The Battle of Coruscant is another unusual space battle, because the same person is giving the orders on both sides! Calling himself Chancellor Palpatine, Darth Sidious is living a double life. As a respected politician, he rules the Galactic Republic, and as the evil Sith Lord, he secretly controls the forces fighting the Republic in the Clone Wars.

To further his own evil schemes, Palpatine makes a very strange order—he demands his henchmen kidnap him on the planet of Coruscant. At his command, a droid army attacks the planet with a huge fleet of ships, and seemingly takes Palpatine prisoner.

As the Sith Lord planned, it falls to Anakin Skywalker and fellow Jedi Obi-Wan Kenobi to rescue their Chancellor in their speedy Jedi Interceptors. In the sky above Coruscant, they fight past a swarm of vicious buzz droids that try to pull their ships apart, and retrieve the Chancellor. If only they knew that he was really a two-faced villain!

A fast, dependable ship can make or break a space battle. Even a little ship like the *Ghost* can make a big difference in the battle against Darth Sidious. This freighter was designed to transport cargo, but it gets its name because it can sneak through the Empire's sensors without being noticed.

The owner and pilot of the *Ghost* is Hera Syndulla—a green-skinned rebel who hates the Empire. She has made her ship a match for the Empire's super-fast TIE fighters!

in battle, the *Ghost* can call on two laser turrets, and has its own small attack shuttle, the *Phantom*, armed with laser cannons and docked at the back of the ship. This is useful when Hera and her friends help out a rebel spy called Tseebo—because a TIE fighter is soon on their tail! They use the *Phantom* to lure the TIE fighter away from the *Ghost* and into an asteroid field. This clever trick gives Hera time to deliver Tseebo to safety before the two ships join up again later.

FLY FOR THE EMPIRE!

Do you hate rebels?
Can you handle a
speedy TIE fighter?

Do you
have quick
reflexes?

**TAKE THE CADET PILOT'S
TEST AND FIND OUT**

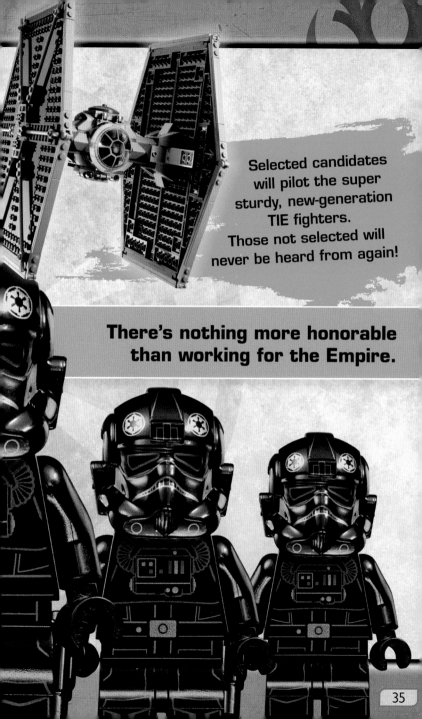

Selected candidates
will pilot the super
sturdy, new-generation
TIE fighters.
Those not selected will
never be heard from again!

**There's nothing more honorable
than working for the Empire.**

Some space battles
require quick thinking and instant
decisions. At the Battle of Yavin, the rebels
come face to face with the Empire's biggest
weapon: the Death Star. They must attack or
be destroyed! As the Death Star heads for the
planet Yavin, its commander, Grand Moff
Tarkin, thinks that it cannot be defeated.
But the rebels know the Death Star has a
weakness: An exhaust vent on its surface
leads directly to the station's reactor core!

The rebels launch their X-wings and Y-wings in the hope of getting just one torpedo into the exhaust. But they are met by TIE fighters and are shot down one by one. Luke Skywalker's X-wing is the rebels' last chance—but the Sith Lord Darth Vader is out in his TIE Advanced, ready to blast him, too! Just in time, Luke's friend Han Solo arrives in his ship, the *Millennium Falcon*, and sends Vader spinning off into space. With Vader out of the way, Luke has just seconds to take the vital shot. It's a hit! The Death Star explodes!

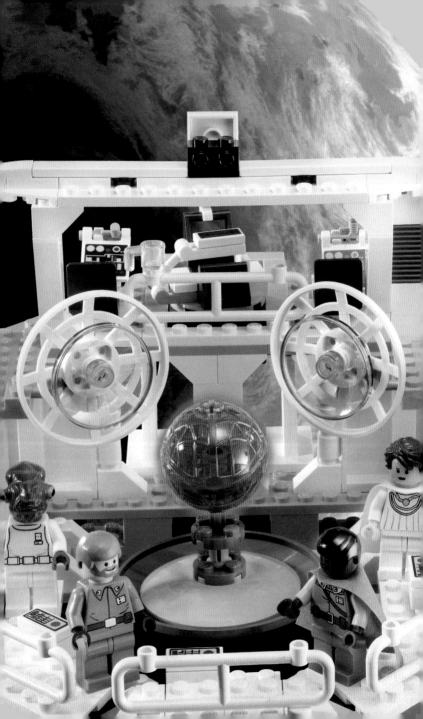

After the Battle of Yavin, Luke and Han
are heroes—but the Empire soon starts work
on a new, better equipped Death Star! This
time, the Emperor and Darth Vader are
taking no chances. They defend the giant
space station with an energy shield generated
on the forest moon of Endor below.

If the rebels are to destroy this Death
Star, they will need to attack on two fronts
and catch the Emperor unaware! So, while
the rebel leaders Mon Mothma and Admiral
Ackbar lead a space attack from their
starcruiser base *Home One*, Han Solo and his
friends attack the shield generator on Endor.

Once the shield is destroyed, the rebels
must act fast! Rebel general Lando
Calrissian flies the *Millennium Falcon* into the
Death Star, bumping and banging through
the vents that lead to the reactor core.

When he arrives he fires a shot that starts
a chain reaction, resulting in the Death
Star exploding. Victory to the rebels!

TACTICAL ANALYSIS
DEATH STAR

This mighty battle station holds many secrets of the Empire. Darth Vader uses the Death Star to destroy starships, discuss battle plans, and hold prisoners. Let's explore!

Whole planets can be blown to bits by this scary superlaser.

The superlaser is fired from this control station.

Watch out for this very powerful turbolaser cannon!

Luke, Chewie, and Leia are about to be squashed as trash!

The Empire's evil plans are hatched in this meeting room.

It's Vader!

These cameras see everything that goes on.

Here's Han Solo in a clever disguise!

This stormtrooper is surprised to see Han on the attack.

Han's dropped his helmet!

Obi-Wan Kenobi is busy shutting down the tractor beam so the rebels can escape.

Stealth Battles

Not all battles are fought with huge armies or war machines. The most important struggles are often behind the scenes.

Palpatine, with his true identity as Darth Sidious, is a master of stealth. He wins battles by manipulating people, often without them even noticing! His rise to power, the creation of his army, and persuading Anakin Skywalker to join the dark side are all achieved by twisting the will of others to fulfill his own evil plans.

The light side uses stealth too, but for different, more honorable, reasons. The Jedi use the power of the Force to disguise their movements, so that they can carry out stealthy investigations. The rebels, fighting alongside the Jedi, learn to master the element of surprise and beat the Empire at its own game. Even a little astromech droid such as R2-D2 can be sent on a secret mission that, if successful, could be a major blow to Palpatine.

The Jedi Master Obi-Wan
Kenobi goes on a secret
mission after uncovering
a plot against Senator
Padmé Amidala.
He must use his
investigative
skills to track down
the attacker, but this only
leads to more mysteries when
a shadowy villain silences
the attacker with a poison dart
before she can say who sent her! And after
learning that the dart comes from the
planet Kamino, Obi-Wan uncovers even
bigger surprises.

The people of Kamino have created a
secret clone army. The clones are copies of
the bounty hunter named Jango Fett.
Obi-Wan suspects that Jango is behind the
assassination attempt and so confronts
him—only to discover that Jango's

weapons are hard to beat. Jango soon escapes aboard his ship, *Slave I*.

Although Obi-Wan loses the fight against Jango, he has uncovered vital information. Thanks to the bounty hunter's Kaminoan dart, the Jedi now know about the secret army on Kamino—and can use it for themselves!

KNOW YOUR WARRIORS
BOUNTY HUNTERS

They hunt down people, and even Sith Lords use their services—they are bounty hunters. For the right price, they will even capture their friends.

BOBA
FETT

PHYSICAL ANALYSIS

"HE'S NO GOOD TO ME DEAD."
BOBA FETT

SPECIAL DEVICE
Rangefinders on helmets help bounty hunters track targets.

ARMOR
Boba's Mandalorian armor is made of tough durasteel.

WEAPON OF CHOICE

Bounty hunters go on missions fraught with dangers. Blaster guns are just what they need for self-protection or to get rid of an enemy.

75%
BATTLE SKILLS

- **KNOWN FOR** Stalking and catching
- **ALLEGIANCE** Anyone who can pay
- **PERSONALITY** Stealthy and clever
- **ENEMIES** Too many to count
- **STRENGTH** Quick reflexes
- **WEAKNESS** Can get overconfident
- **WATCH OUT FOR** Sudden strikes

• BATTLE STORY •

Han Solo has a bounty on his head. Greedo, a bounty hunter from Tatooine, finds him first. Han, however, proves too clever for Greedo. But Darth Vader outwits him and hands him over to Boba.

The Jedi should be suspicious of their new clone army—the true hand behind its creation is Palpatine! The Sith Lord's rise to power, from senator to Chancellor—the most important job in the Republic—is through decades of clever, patient planning, and is the stealthiest work in all the galaxy.

Palpatine engineers a war in the galaxy to weaken the Jedi and make people believe that they need a powerful Emperor to bring order to their worlds again. He then uses his clones to destroy the Jedi, thus eliminating his only threat.

Palpatine's biggest weapon is the angry, greedy Jedi Anakin Skywalker. Palpatine persuades Anakin to give in to his emotions and become the all-powerful Sith Lord Darth Vader. With his help, Palpatine achieves his ultimate goal of being made Emperor.

Yet stealthy Palpatine makes one big mistake! He does not know about Anakin's twin children, born in secret. One day they might be his undoing!

ORDER 66
HOW IT HAPPENED

Darth Sidious issued Order 66, a secret instruction to destroy all the Jedi. Afterwards, there was nobody left to challenge Sidious and he could make himself Emperor!

WHO DID WHAT?

Darth Sidious

This devious politician waited years to strike. With Order 66 he finally is rid of the Jedi.

Clone Troopers

The clone troopers received a secret message ordering them to destroy the Jedi that they were protecting.

Anakin Skywalker

Anakin secretly joined Sidious. He destroyed the Jedi Temple and all the young Padawans, too.

On Kashyyyk, Jedi Grand Master Yoda battled Commander Gree. The experienced Jedi destroyed the clone officer and escaped.

Commander Cody almost destroyed Obi-Wan Kenobi on planet Utapau, but the Jedi Master managed a quick getaway.

MESSAGE OF HOPE

Obi-Wan Kenobi sent out a message warning any surviving Jedi to hide. The Empire will never stop looking for them.

"Our Jedi Order and the Republic have fallen—with the dark shadow of Empire rising to take their place."

"Do not return to the temple... that time has passed and our future is uncertain..."

In a galaxy full of important people like Emperor Palpatine, little astromech droids can pass by entirely unnoticed. The rebel Princess Leia is desperate, but also clever when she sends her droid R2-D2 on a top-secret mission.

Leia has learned about the Empire's Death Star. She has also managed to steal the plans! But she is in danger and needs to send a message to people who can stop the Empire. She knows of someone who can help—Obi-Wan Kenobi. He is hiding on Tatooine, so she sends R2-D2 to find him.

R2-D2 is brave and determined. It's not easy for a droid to wheel across Tatooine's sand, but he doesn't give up! Not even being captured by junk-collecting Jawas deters him from his mission. A bit of luck helps, too: His droid friend C-3PO persuades moisture farmer Owen Lars and his nephew, Luke Skywalker, to buy the pair of them from the Jawas. It is Luke who inadvertently leads R2-D2 to Obi-Wan, who has been watching from nearby. R2-D2 then reveals Leia's message, which he has been carefully hiding the whole time!

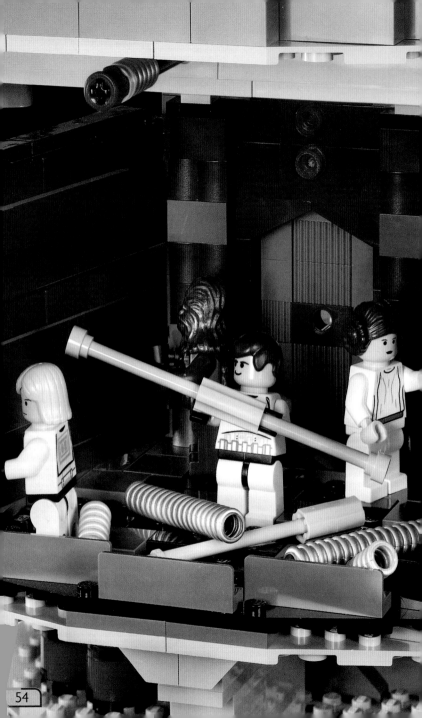

Not all secret missions go as planned. Sometimes the rebels' schemes go awry, and then they need quick thinking and teamwork to escape tricky situations.

When Luke Skywalker, Han Solo, and Chewbacca join Obi-Wan Kenobi's mission to rescue Princess Leia from the Death Star, the two humans plan to go undercover by disguising themselves as stormtoopers! The rescue is successful, but on the way back to Han's ship, the *Millennium Falcon*, they are forced to hide from some real stormtroopers in a trash compactor. When the compactor is suddenly turned on, they are nearly crushed. Thankfully they have back-up: C-3PO and R2-D2 are able to shut the compactor down.

The friends all meet back at the *Millennium Falcon* but watch helplessly as Darth Vader strikes down Obi-Wan Kenobi. They manage to escape because Obi-Wan distracted the Sith Lord for them. They know that Obi-Wan lost this battle to help them get away.

Man vs. Machine

A leader is more powerful with an army at his back—and even more so with a mechanical one. In large numbers, droids are a powerful threat and can conquer many worlds. They are programmed to carry out orders without question and their shells are armored against attack. Smaller droids are useful to the Empire as spies and probes, searching for signs of rebel activity.

However, machines are unable to win the bigger war, due to their lesser intelligence and inability to adapt to new situations. They rely on yet more machines to give them instructions, such as their control ships or tactical droids. What a mistake!

The danger for the Empire is that they will come to rely too heavily on their mechanical soldiers. The Jedi and rebels' belief in fighting for freedom, and ability to think creatively, prevents the droids from winning on many occasions.

Most machines can be destroyed with skill and strategy, or even by a boy in a starfighter strong in the Force, but some are more difficult to destroy than others…

©LEGO

The Jedi are trained to fight all kinds of foes, including mechanical ones! However, some machines are well equipped to defend themselves—even against lightsabers.

When the planet Naboo is threatened with invasion by the greedy Trade Federation, Obi-Wan Kenobi and his fellow Jedi Qui-Gon Jinn are sent to help find a peaceful solution. But Darth Sidious is secretly controlling the Trade Federation and he does not want peace! Battle droids are sent to attack Obi-Wan and Qui-Gon, and the Jedi quickly defeat these simple machines. But then some much more powerful droidekas show up!

Droidekas are far more powerful than normal droids. They can roll up into a ball and move very fast. They also have protective energy shields and very effective blaster cannons.

At first, Obi-Wan and Qui-Gon can repel the droidekas' blasts with their lightsabers, but even Jedi get tired eventually—unlike robots. There is only one thing left to do: flee! A Jedi that knows when to retreat lives to fight another day.

A vast mechanical army defends the villainous Poggle the Lesser on the planet Geonosis. When Poggle captures Obi-Wan Kenobi, Anakin Skywalker, and Padmé Amidala, the Galactic Republic sends its own army of clones to rescue them. Both armies are well matched with war machines: The clones have AT-TE tanks and gunships armed with laser cannons and missiles, and their opponents are hailfire droids, spindly spider droids, and chunky tank droids.

The droids fight particularly well on Geonosis, because this is the terrain on which they were designed and tested. However, the clones have an advantage. They may be copies, but they still think as individuals and can adapt to new conditions in the middle of the action. Eventually, the Jedi's clone troopers win the Battle of Geonosis. If only Yoda knew that the clones were not truly loyal to the Jedi—but instead programmed to obey Darth Sidious!

As part of his training to become a Jedi and be ready to fight the Empire, Luke Skywalker uses machines for his own benefit. Aboard the *Millennium Falcon*, Luke practices lightsaber techniques with a training remote droid. Obi-Wan knows that it is best to rely on the Force, so he makes Luke wear a helmet that blocks his vision. Even without his sight, Luke successfully blocks the flying remote's blaster fire with his lightsaber—he is learning to use the Force!

On the planet Dagobah, Luke learns from Yoda that no machine, however big or small, is a match for the power of the Force. When Luke's X-wing sinks into the swamp, Master Yoda tells him to levitate it! Luke is intimidated by the X-wing's large size. He is therefore surprised when little Yoda succeeds in lifting it out of the water. Luke said he would try, but he didn't really believe he could do it. Yoda teaches him to believe in his own abilities in order to succeed.

When the rebels, including Luke and Han, go into hiding on the frozen world of Hoth, the Empire searches high and low across the galaxy to find them—sending out probe droids that are built for spy missions.

So, when Han and Chewbacca think they see a meteor strike outside their secret base, they should be very careful! The meteor turns out to be a probe droid, which records information about the planet and sends it back to Darth Vader. The droid defends itself by firing at Han and Chewie, but when they fire back, it explodes. The droid's mission is successful because it finds the rebels and doesn't let itself be captured.

The Empire soon arrives above Hoth with its Star Destroyers, but the officer in charge doesn't do his job as well as the probe droid. He brings the fleet out of hyperspace much too close to Hoth. His poor strategy alerts the rebels and ruins the Empire's opportunity for a surprise attack... and this makes Darth Vader very angry!

TACTICAL ANALYSIS
AT-AT ATTACK

Rebels beware! The Empire has sent one of
its best war machines on a mission to Hoth.
Equipped with advanced
weapons, the AT-AT Walker
is built to seek and destroy.

**This flexible neck
helps weapons to fire
in all directions.**

**Rebels should
steer clear of
these fearsome
laser cannons.**

**A blaster bolt
on its way to its
unlucky target!**

**Pilot gets a good view
from his high cockpit.**

Armored side hatch opens up to deploy troops.

Snowtroopers wear special gear for chilly Hoth. Brrr!

Feet and legs are strong but can be tripped up.

Mind Wars

It doesn't matter how many planets you conquer or how big your army is—no war is ever really over until you win the battle of the mind. The evil Sith are experts at this kind of warfare. They use trickery and lies to make people think differently. The Jedi have mind tricks of their own, but they use them with care not to do any harm. In fact, mind wars can be found everywhere in the galaxy. Even Padmé Amidala convincing the Gungans to join her fight against an army of droids is a battle to decide the best thing to do.

Some mind wars are very brief, like when Darth Vader uses threats to make Princess Leia tell him where the rebels are hiding (he fails). Others last for years, like when Darth Sidious slowly lures Anakin Skywalker over to the dark side (he succeeds). The scary thing is, you might not even know when a mind war is happening!

FACE-OFF
Jedi Master vs. Sith Lord

Palpatine's secret is out. Mace Windu knows he is a Sith. But the Chancellor will not go down without a fight.

"You are under arrest, Chancellor!"

Mace Windu, Jedi Master

- **Strengths** Wise, master swordsman
- **Weakness** Too arrogant
- **Weapon** Purple lightsaber

"Are you threatening me, Master Jedi?"

Palpatine, Sith Lord

- **Strength** Dark side of the Force
- **Weakness** Underestimates the light side
- **Weapon** Force lightning, red lightsaber

When Anakin Skywalker turns to the dark side, it comes as a surprise to his Jedi friends. Master Yoda senses fear in him, but he does not know that Anakin's biggest fear is that something bad will happen to Padmé.

As a Sith Lord, Darth Sidious knows all about using people's fear against them. For years, he has tricked people into thinking he can protect them from problems that he has been secretly causing.

Sidious knows that Anakin is very worried about Padmé, so he tells him that the only way to protect her is to use the dark side of the Force.

Anakin does not want to join the dark side, but Sidious is a very

convincing liar. He makes Anakin think that he has no choice! So Anakin joins forces with Darth Sidious and helps him defeat Jedi Master Mace Windu.

There is no way back for Anakin now. His fear has become anger. Perhaps he could have defeated Darth Sidious in a lightsaber battle, but instead he has been beaten with clever words. He has turned his back on the Jedi and become a Sith!

When Anakin Skywalker turns to the
dark side, he takes a new name: Darth
Vader! It is exactly what Darth Sidious
wanted. Now nothing can stop them from
creating an Empire to rule the galaxy!

One of the planets in this new Empire
is Lothal. The people who live there don't
like Darth Sidious or Darth Vader, and
a group of rebels does its best to make life
hard for their evil rulers.

The Empire must fight a constant battle
to keep the people under control, so every

year they hold an event called Empire Day. This grand military parade of stormtroopers and AT-DP walkers looks like a celebration, but it is really meant to show everyone just how powerful the Empire is. It is a kind of mind war called propaganda. Over time, it is designed to change the way people think!

The rebels of Lothal know that the best way to fight the empire's propaganda is with a clear message of their own. So they attack the parade to make it look weak, and write messages of resistance wherever they go.

Even the Jedi play mind games from time to time! Unlike the Sith, they are careful not to abuse their powers—but a Jedi mind trick can be very useful for getting out of a sticky situation without using a lightsaber!

On Tatooine, Obi-Wan Kenobi, C-3PO, and Luke Skywalker are on a mission to smuggle R2-D2 to the Rebel Alliance when they are stopped by two sandtroopers. These special stormtroopers have been warned to watch out for droids, and there's no hiding R2-D2 and C-3PO! Luckily, the sandtroopers are not very strong-minded and Obi-Wan is able to plant a suggestion in their minds using the Force. "These are not the droids you're looking for," he tells them with a wave of his hand. "These are not the droids we're looking for," they agree!

Things aren't so easy when Obi-Wan tries to use his mind tricks on an angry customer in the Mos Eisley Cantina —his mind is too strong with rage. That's when having a lightsaber also comes in handy!

KNOW YOUR WARRIORS
SITH

The Force is strong in the Sith and they use it to destroy all those who defy them. They lurk in the shadows making sneaky plans to take over the galaxy.

DARTH VADER

PHYSICAL ANALYSIS

VADER'S MASK
Filter helps with breathing and also makes a scary sound.

SPECIAL SUIT
Complex mesh of wires and buttons keeps Vader alive.

"DON'T MAKE ME DESTROY YOU!"
DARTH VADER

WEAPON OF CHOICE

Beware a Sith wielding a red-bladed lightsaber. Darth Vader can swing his with fierce speed, and Darth Maul's has two blades for double the trouble!

95%
BATTLE SKILLS

▶ **KNOWN FOR** Unjust rule

▶ **ALLEGIANCE** To themselves

▶ **PERSONALITY** Evil, cunning

▶ **ENEMIES** Jedi, Rebel Alliance

▶ **STRENGTH** Imperial army, the Force

▶ **WEAKNESS** Greed for power

▶ **WATCH OUT FOR** Force choke

• BATTLE STORY •
Sith Lord Darth Vader shows no mercy. Especially if it's an Imperial officer who has allowed the rebels to escape, yet again! Like the time Vader destroyed Admiral Ozzel for allowing the rebels to escape from the planet Hoth.

Darth Sidious was very pleased with himself when he lured Anakin Skywalker to the dark side and turned him into Darth Vader. So it's no surprise when he tries to do the same thing with Anakin's son, Luke!

The sneaky Sith uses lots of different mind tricks to convince Luke to join him. First, he tries to make Luke lose hope by telling him that his friends are doomed. Then he makes Luke angry, in the hope that his rage will take him over. Finally, he manipulates Luke into fighting Vader, but Luke will not give in to his rage and destroy his father.

When Sidious sees that his plan is not working, he turns to violence— shooting Force lightning from his fingers at Luke! But Vader cannot stand by and see his son destroyed. So he picks up Darth Sidious and hurls him deep into the reactor core of the Death Star, never to be seen again!

Darth Sidious's devious
mind war has succeeded
in changing the mind
of a Skywalker—it's
just not the change
he expected!

Nature's Dangers

Battles don't have to be between Sith and Jedi. Some of the toughest struggles are against something even Darth Sidious can't control: nature itself!

The sandstorms on the dry, desert planet of Tatooine, snow blizzards on icy Hoth, and the fiery lava of Mustafar can be just as menacing as an AT-AT. Worse still are some of the ferocious creatures that live across the galaxy—a cyborg wielding a lightsaber may not be as threatening as the bad-tempered rancor kept in Jabba the Hutt's dungeon, or a giant, hungry wampa on Hoth. And the thought of being swallowed by the terrifying Sarlacc on Tatooine is enough to scare even the meanest bounty hunter.

Survival often means learning to work with nature, rather than against it. In the maze-like forests of Endor, the rebels must quickly learn how to work with the furry Ewoks, or risk being eaten in a sacrificial ceremony! And when Obi-Wan Kenobi battles Anakin Skywalker on Mustafar, he must dodge blows from his former apprentice at the same time as trying not to fall into the scorching-hot lava beneath them.

When the rebels pick Hoth as a base to hide from the Empire, they don't choose it for its climate! The icy temperatures are cold enough to freeze rebels, so they must wrap up warm. In order to check the surroundings for any signs of spies from the Empire, the rebels ride smelly but harmless creatures called tauntauns, who have wide feet for trekking through Hoth's deep snowdrifts. But, as Luke Skywalker discovers, there are bigger dangers than snow and ice around!

Tauntauns are the favorite snack of another creature well-adapted to the cold of Hoth: the wampa. Luke must fight for his life when he and his tauntaun are snatched by the huge, clawed paws of one of these hungry beasts. The wampa begins to eat the tauntaun, but keeps Luke hanging upside-down in his cave as an ice-cold dessert for later!

Using the Force, Luke manages to grab his lightsaber. With one swing he injures the monster and makes a quick escape. Phew!

A HOT DUEL
Obi-Wan takes on his former Padawan, Anakin, on the scorching planet of Mustafar. Both engage in a fierce duel, as they dodge fiery splatters of lava.

FACE-OFF
Jedi Knight vs. Hungry Beast

Luke Skywalker finds himself facing a hungry rancor. He must act fast before the beast turns him into lunch.

"Uh-oh!!"

Luke Skywalker, Jedi

- **Strength** Quick thinking
- **Weakness** Missing lightsaber
- **Weapon** Discarded bone

"Grrrrrrr!"

Rancor, Hungry Beast

- **Strength** Massive, scary size
- **Weakness** Slow reflexes
- **Weapons** Razor-sharp teeth and claws

Hoth is not the only place Luke must battle a fierce beast. On his home planet of Tatooine, during a mission to free his captured friend, Han Solo, he comes face-to-face with a toothy, strong-armed rancor.

In their natural habitat, rancors would not attack people, but this one is being kept as a pet in a dingy dungeon belonging to crime lord Jabba the Hutt. So when Luke falls into his cell, the creature charges straight at him!

Luke landed in this mess by trying to use Jedi mind tricks to force Jabba to release Han. But mind tricks don't work on Hutts, and Jabba drops Luke into his rancor pit. Without his lightsaber, Luke grabs a bone instead and jams it into the rancor's open jaws. It's a simple trick, but it works, and the rancor drops him! Luke then traps the creature beneath the heavy door of its cage—finishing it off once and for all! Luke's quick thinking and quicker actions helped him beat the rancor.

The death of his rancor makes Jabba very cranky! Unluckily for Luke Skywalker, Han Solo, and Princess Leia, Jabba has other pets that like to eat his prisoners. Out in the

Tatooine desert, Jabba knows of something worse than a rancor—a Sarlacc! Sarlaccs are rare, tentacled monsters that eat anything. This one hides most of its cavernous body deep beneath the sand. Jabba is excited by the thought of feeding the rebels to this hideous creature and prepares a party for the occasion!

However, Jabba doesn't know that his new slave droid R2-D2 is hiding Luke's lightsaber, and is ready to launch it toward Luke at just the right moment! Nor does Jabba know that one of his thugs is Han's friend Lando Calrissian in disguise. Acting fast, Luke and Lando knock Jabba's henchmen into the mouth of the Sarlacc. Meanwhile, Leia holds Jabba back with a chain and the rebels are free! The Sarlacc might be even happier than the heroes—it gets to eat all of Jabba's men!

TACTICAL ANALYSIS
JABBA'S BARGE

Jabba the Hutt is off to the Great Pit of Carkoon to throw prisoners into the Sarlacc's mouth. Until then, there's always live music and good food aboard his sail barge—the *Khettana*.

Sails protect from the sun and help with sailing.

Hidden pirate cannon always catches attackers by surprise.

Uncomfortable cells for prisoners waiting to be fed to the Sarlacc.

Slimy Jabba loves tormenting his prisoners.

Weequay guard keeps an eye out for surprise attacks.

Max Rebo plays Jabba's favorite tunes.

Princess Leia is forced to wear a slave outfit.

Side-walls fold down to protect passengers.

Big, toothy monsters are scary, but small creatures pose a threat, too. The rebels learn that to survive in Endor's forest, and defeat the Empire, they must befriend the natives.

Soon after landing on Endor, Han, Luke, Chewbacca, C-3PO, and R2-D2 are captured by Ewoks. The furry Ewoks look small and innocent, but they tie up the rebels and take them to their village for dinner—where the heroes are the ones on the menu! Luke has to think fast to persuade the Ewoks to let them go, and join their fight against the Empire. With stormtroopers invading the Ewoks' home, the little creatures quickly agree.

The Ewoks use simple catapults and gliders, and even sticks and stones, to fight the Empire's forces. Although their technology is primitive, they are able to win the battle because they are fighting in familiar surroundings and know the best routes through the trees. The Empire's forces are surprised by the Ewoks' creativity and persistence. They also underestimate the little creatures' strength!

Mighty Duels

The vast wars waged across the galaxy often hinge upon duels fought between individual Sith and Jedi. Unlike ground or space battles, with their huge armies of droids and soldiers, these tightly fought battles are contested one-on-one and depend on focus and skill more than strength or size.

The Sith are fierce opponents, but as there are only ever two of them at one time, they must choose their battles carefully. The Sith fight alone and have no friends, but a Sith Master will always train an apprentice to take over in case they are defeated.

A duel with a Sith can be full of surprises: Count Dooku, for example, will resort to nasty tricks if things don't go his way. Darth Vader, on the other hand, appears unstoppable—even after sustaining dreadful injuries on Mustafar, he returns to duel again!

Jedi must learn how to duel early in their training. During the Battle of Naboo, Obi-Wan Kenobi is still a young trainee Jedi, but he is still able to defeat Darth Sidious's evil apprentice, Darth Maul.

Darth Sidious sends Maul to ambush Qui-Gon Jinn and Obi-Wan Kenobi. Armed with a double-bladed lightsaber, Maul can fight both Jedi at once! He starts by knocking Obi-Wan down, at which point the young Jedi becomes separated from his Master, Qui-Gon. Obi-Wan can only watch as Maul uses his superior skills to defeat Qui-Gon.

As soon as he is able, Obi-Wan attacks and he and Maul clash furiously. It looks like Maul will win, as Obi-Wan loses his lightsaber and finds himself hanging perilously from a ledge! Maul stands above, taunting him, but Obi-Wan remains calm and concentrates. By using the Force, he summons Qui-Gon's lightsaber, then launches himself up out of the pit. He lands behind Maul and swings the lightsaber. The Sith tumbles down the shaft, defeated! Maul was the better fighter, but his arrogance made him sloppy. In this duel, Obi-Wan's focus gave him the advantage.

Sometimes a Jedi Master has to fight his former Padawan. Count Dooku was once Yoda's student, but he left the light side behind to join Darth Sidious. Yoda knows how dangerous he is, but as a battle rages on Geonosis, it is Anakin and Obi-Wan who rashly decide to confront the Sith. Anakin is overconfident and charges Dooku first. The inexperienced Padawan is quickly injured and blasted against the wall. Obi-Wan is not strong enough to take

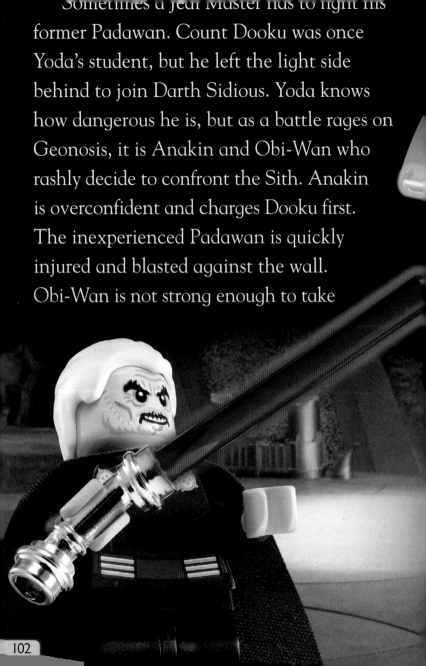

on the Sith by himself either and on this
occasion is quickly knocked out.

The Jedi's inability to work together is their
downfall. It is Yoda who comes to their aid.
Dooku greets his former Master by aiming
Force lightning at him. Yoda is able to protect
himself and soon the two begin to duel!

The more experienced Yoda might have
won the fight, but Dooku fights dirty. He tries
to pull a column down on Anakin and
Obi-Wan, knowing Yoda will rush to save his
fellow Jedi. This time, Dooku escapes.

FACE-OFF

Cyborg vs. Jedi Master

Cyber villain General Grievous wants to destroy all the Jedi. It's up to Obi-Wan Kenobi to stop him.

"You are doomed!"

General Grievous, Evil Cyborg

- **Strength** Tough metal body with four arms
- **Weakness** Overconfidence
- **Weapons** Lightsabers stolen from the Jedi

Obi-Wan Kenobi,
Jedi Master

- **Strength** Jedi skills, the Force
- **Weakness** Has only two arms
- **Weapons** Lightsaber, blaster gun

"Oh, I don't think so!"

After Darth Sidious orders the destruction of all the Jedi, any Jedi left are scattered far across the galaxy. Yoda is one of the few to escape. He knows that he has one last chance to take on Darth Sidious himself.

Yoda arrives at the Emperor's senate office and confronts him, but Sidious blasts Yoda with Force lightning, sending him flying across the room. As Sidious approaches, Yoda draws his green lightsaber and the two begin dueling fiercely. Like all Sith, Sidious uses dirty tricks, and begins hurling obstacles at Yoda through the power of the Force. But Yoda is also powerful, and is able to fling objects back at Sidious! The Sith blasts Yoda with another volley of lightning, but Yoda blocks it, and the blast of Force energy sends them both falling to the ground.

Yoda has met his match! He is not strong enough to defeat the Emperor. No remaining Jedi is. Yoda realizes that he and Obi-Wan must go into hiding and wait for a new hope to fight Sidious...

When a Jedi falls to the dark side, he becomes an enemy and a threat to the people who were his friends. So when Anakin joins the Sith as Darth Sidious's apprentice, his former Master, Obi-Wan, knows he must try to stop him in any way possible.

Obi-Wan tracks Anakin to the volcanic planet of Mustafar. Neither will surrender nor let the other walk away, so they draw their lightsabers to begin an epic battle. Jumping across mining platforms, they duel their way through lava flows and fiery blasts.

The two Jedi are nearly equally matched. It's impossible to determine who might win, until Obi-Wan lands on higher ground— out of the reach of Anakin's lightsaber. Anakin has become so arrogant and blinded by rage that he has lost his ability to sense when he should withdraw. Instead, he leaps toward Obi-Wan. With one swing of his lightsaber, Obi-Wan knocks out Anakin and injures him. Due to his own decision to abandon the light side, Anakin loses the duel and nearly his life in the fires of Mustafar.

Rebels Kanan and Ezra meet a strange new enemy in a three-way duel on the planet Stygeon Prime. They arrive with the hope of rescuing a Jedi that they believe is being held prisoner there, but instead discover that they have been lured into a trap!

They are greeted by a pale villain who introduces himself as the Inquisitor and draws his lightsaber to duel. The Inquisitor is not a Sith, but serves the Sith and has learned their ways. Kanan has been training Ezra as a Jedi, but the two quickly discover that the Inquisitor is too strong for them. Whenever Kanan manages to strike back, the Inquisitor blocks his lightsaber with ease. When the rebels run, the Inquisitor follows!

The Inquisitor tries to separate Kanan from Ezra, but the pair dive through closing doors and escape. Kanan knows they only got away because the Inquisitor toyed with them, rather than defeating them when he had the chance. Further Jedi training is essential!

After defeating Anakin on Mustafar, Obi-Wan thought he would never face him again. But aboard the Death Star, the Jedi must duel with him one last time.

As Darth Vader, Anakin has lost some of his powers—but his machine body helps him and he senses Obi-Wan's arrival. When they last met, Anakin was much less experienced. Now, the Sith has become stronger, while Obi-Wan has grown old.

As they fight, Obi-Wan knows he cannot defeat Vader, and has no way to escape. Obi-Wan is old and out of practice. But he can distract Vader, giving his friends more time to flee. When he sees that Luke and the others have reached the *Millennium Falcon* and can fly to safety, Obi-Wan knows his mission is over, so he surrenders. Vader strikes his former Master and destroys him. He thinks he has won. But Obi-Wan has become more powerful than Vader can imagine, as a blue, glowing Force spirit.

Darth Vader has personal reasons for seeking a duel with Luke Skywalker. The cunning Sith Lord uses Luke's friends as bait to lure him to Cloud City. Luke does come, although he might have made a mistake in not finishing his Jedi training with Yoda on Dagobah first. In the end, it is Luke, and not his friends, who needs rescuing!

When Luke arrives, Vader confronts him and the two begin to fight. Vader is the stronger, and traps Luke at the core of the

city, above a deep shaft. As the battle continues, Luke is badly injured by Vader.

Luke is now helpless, but Vader has one more surprise: He reveals that he is Luke's father and tempts him to join the dark side! Luke refuses and escapes by jumping down the shaft. Under Cloud City, he hangs on for dear life, until Leia returns with the *Millennium Falcon* to pick him up. Luke learns that next time he should be better trained before going off to save his friends, or the galaxy!

The next time that Luke Skywalker faces Darth Vader it is in a duel planned by Darth Sidious. In pitting father and son against each other, Sidious hopes that Luke will destroy Vader and become his new Sith apprentice! However, for Sidious, it all goes wrong.

Luke has learned from their previous duel and his renewed training has made him just as powerful as Darth Vader. As their lightsabers clash, Luke gives in to anger and attacks Vader furiously. Luke realizes that if he continues, he will be no better than Vader himself. Luke refuses to fight his father any more, hoping instead that Vader is not fully lost to the dark side.

Sidious is furious when Luke refuses to fight and zaps him with Force lightning. But Luke is right about his father, and Vader comes to his rescue. The two Sith Lords struggle and both are destroyed. The dark side is defeated!

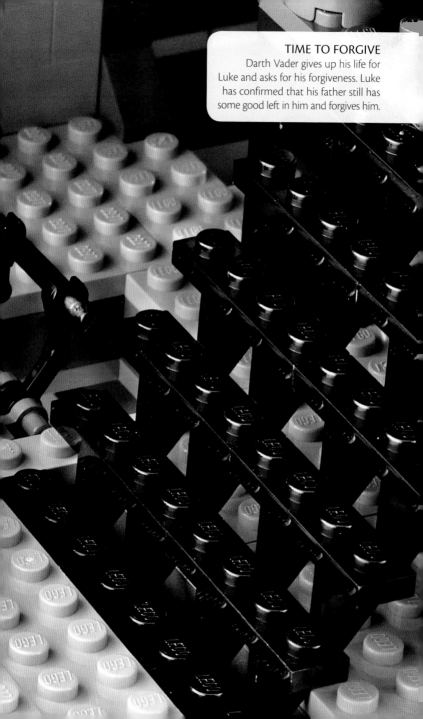

TIME TO FORGIVE
Darth Vader gives up his life for Luke and asks for his forgiveness. Luke has confirmed that his father still has some good left in him and forgives him.

KNOW YOUR WARRIORS
IMPERIAL SOLDIERS

The loyal soldiers of the Empire will blindly follow Imperial orders—no questions asked. They also love to bully common citizens across the galaxy.

STORMTROOPER

PHYSICAL ANALYSIS

HELMETS
Stormtrooper helmets come equipped with air vents and holocams.

ARMOR
Tough armor can withstand pistol shots and heavy battle fire.

"REBELS! BLAST 'EM."
STORMTROOPER

WEAPON OF CHOICE

Blaster rifles are stormtroopers' standard weapons. These fully automatic blasters can shoot pulse beams for up to 300 meters.

45%
BATTLE SKILLS

▶ **KNOWN FOR** Enforcing unjust rules

▶ **ALLEGIANCE** The Empire

▶ **PERSONALITY** Cold, emotionless

▶ **ENEMIES** Those fighting the Empire

▶ **STRENGTH** Strict Imperial training

▶ **WEAKNESS** Can't make decisions

▶ **WATCH OUT FOR** Mass attacks

• BATTLE STORY •

The Empire spends years training the stormtroopers. Academies across the galaxy put them through rigorous training and condition their brains to obey Imperial orders. As a result stormtroopers can't make good decisions.

Quiz

1. Who is Obi-Wan Kenobi's Jedi Master?

2. On what planet does Obi-Wan discover the clone army?

3. Where was Palpatine born?

4. What is the name of the command that Palpatine gives to destroy all the Jedi?

5. Which droid carries a special message to Tatooine for Princess Leia?

6. What type of droid discovers the rebels and their secret base on Hoth?

7. What creature do wampas like to eat?

8. What is the main weakness of an AT-AT?

9. What simple weapon does Luke Skywalker use to distract the rancor?

10. What is the name of Hera Syndulla's ship?

11. Which planet is covered in fire and lava?

12. How do Luke Skywalker and Han Solo disguise themselves to rescue Princess Leia?

13. Who do Kanan and Ezra meet on the planet Stygeon Prime?

14. Which rebel destroys the first Death Star?

15. Where is Darth Sidious finally defeated?

See page 127 for answers

Glossary

Awry
Gone wrong, not according to plan.

Betrayed
Behaved in a disloyal way, broke another person's trust.

Bounty hunter
Someone who hunts down other people for a reward, often money.

Chancellor
Important and powerful politician.

Clone
Identical copy of another person or object.

Cyborg
Living being whose body is made up of some robotic parts.

Droid
Metal robot.

Empire
Group of worlds ruled over by one leader, called an Emperor.

Galaxy
Group of millions of stars and planets.

Generator
Machine that creates power, usually electrical.

Imperial
Belonging to the Empire.

Jedi
Someone who uses the Force to protect people and keep the peace.

Levitate
Make something hover in the air, above the ground.

Lightsaber
A weapon made of pure Force energy, used in battles like a sword.

Lure
Persuade someone to go somewhere or do something with a promise of a reward.

Manipulate
Influence a person or situation for your own benefit.

Menace
A threat. Something likely to cause harm.

Primitive
Not very technologically advanced, basic.

Propaganda
Information used to persuade people to believe something that might not be true—often for political reasons.

Rebel
Person who rises up to fight against the current rulers.

Republic
Nation, or nations, where the people vote for their leaders.

Senate
Group of people who rule the Republic together.

Sith
Someone who uses the Force for selfish reasons and to gain power.

Stealthy
Able to act quietly and secretly, without anybody noticing.

Swarm
Large group that moves around together, often flying.

Terrain
Stretch of ground.

Underestimate
To mistakenly think somebody else is not capable of something.

Index

Quiz answers:
1. Qui-Gon Jinn 2. Kamino 3. On the planet Naboo 4. Order 66
5. R2-D2 6. A probe droid 7. Tauntauns 8. Its legs 9. A bone
10. The *Ghost* 11. Mustafar 12. They dress up as stormtroopers
13. The Inquisitor 14. Luke Skywalker 15. The Death Star

DK ADVENTURES

Experience ancient Roman intrigue in this time-traveling adventure.

It's a life-or-death mission as the gang searches for a new home planet.

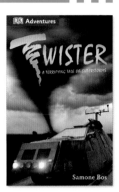

Chase twisters in Tornado Alley in this pulse-racing action book.

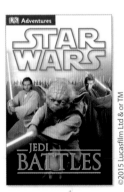

Find out all about the brave Jedi Knights and their epic adventures.

Meet the Sith Lords who are trying to take over the galaxy.

Read all about the scariest monsters in the *Star Wars* galaxy.